W9-BWG-320

Air Sports

Andrew Luke

MASON CREST

Air Sports

Andrew Luke

MC

MASON CREST

MASON CREST
450 Parkway Drive, Suite D
Broomall, Pennsylvania 19008
(866) MCP-BOOK (toll-free)

Andrew Luke

First printing
9 8 7 6 5 4 3 2 1

ISBN (hardback) 978-1-4222-3705-2
ISBN (series) 978-1-4222-3704-5
ISBN (ebook) 978-1-4222-8078-2

Cover and Interior designed by Tara Raymo; www.creativelytara.com

Cataloging-in-Publication Data on file with the Library of Congress

QR CODES AND LINKS TO THIRD-PARTY CONTENT
You may gain access to certain third-party content ("Third-Party Sites") by scanning and using the QR Codes that appear in this publication (the "QR Codes"). We do not operate or control in any respect any information, products, or services on such Third-Party Sites linked to by us via the QR Codes included in this publication, and we assume no responsibility for any materials you may access using the QR Codes. Your use of the QR Codes may be subject to terms, limitations or restrictions set forth in the applicable terms of use or otherwise established by the owners of the Third-Party Sites. Our linking to such Third-Party Sites via the QR Codes does not imply an endorsement or sponsorship of such Third-Party Sites, or the information, products, or services offered on or through the Third- Party Sites, nor does it imply an endorsement or sponsorship of this publication by the owners of such Third-Party Sites.

Table of Contents

Key icons to look for:

Words to Understand: These words with their easy-to-understand definitions will increase the reader's understanding of the text while building vocabulary skills.

Text-Dependent Questions: These questions send the reader back to the text for more careful attention to the evidence presented there.

Sidebars: This boxed material within the main text allows readers to build knowledge, gain insights, explore possibilities, and broaden their perspectives by weaving together additional information to provide realistic and holistic perspectives.

Research Projects: Readers are pointed toward areas of further inquiry connected to each chapter. Suggestions are provided for projects that encourage deeper research and analysis.

Educational Videos: Readers can view videos by scanning our QR codes, providing them with additional educational content to supplement the text. Examples include news coverage, moments in history, speeches, iconic sports moments and much more!

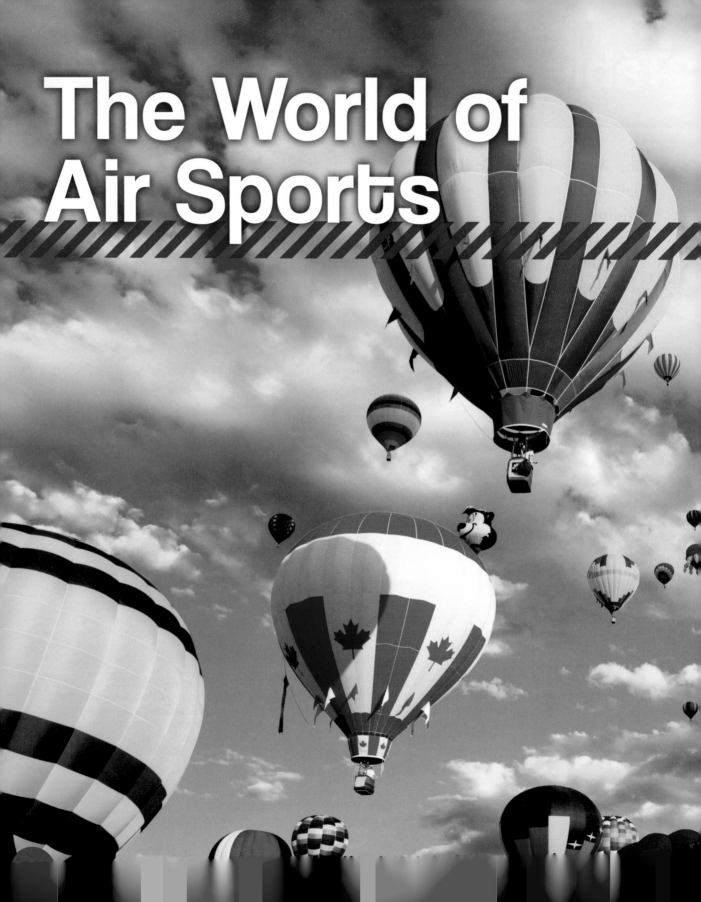

The World of
Air Sports

Human flight is a relatively new phenomenon in the world. The desire of humans to fly, however, has existed for centuries. Early attempts at flying, dating back to the sixth century in China and the ninth century in Europe, were disastrous and often deadly.

These attempts ranged from jumping off towers attached to a pair of man-made wings to trying to hold onto giant kites. Without a proper understanding of aerodynamics and the science of flight, success was impossible to find.

The first true breakthrough in terms of actually moving people through the air in a controlled way came in France in 1783, when inventors were able to get hot air-filled balloons to carry passengers for several kilometers in an attached basket. The most successful flight lasted more than 2 hours and covered 36 km (22 miles).

Hot air balloons were very popular in the 19th century, and electric-powered blimps were also developed in the late 1800s, with the most well-known examples designed by German Ferdinand von Zeppelin, whose first airship took flight in 1900.

In 1905, the World Air Sports Federation (officially the Fédération Aéronautique Internationale [FAI] in French) was founded in Switzerland to govern aeronautical activities, or all activities concerned with flying. Today the FAI governs everything from ballooning and gliding to microlighting and airplanes and runs the World Air Games, a multidisciplinary air sports competition event held every 4 years.

Power Outage

There are two basic categories of air sports: with power and without power. Air sports can also be categorized as lighter or heavier than air.

Ballooning

Words to Understand

accurately: free from error or defect; consistent with a standard, rule, or model; precise; exact.

mastered: having become adept in something.

predetermined: settled or decided in advance.

Hot air balloons fall into both the no power and lighter-than-air categories. They work based on the simple fact that hot air is lighter than cold air. Therefore, when the air inside the balloon is heated, it begins to float. When early balloonists **mastered** this concept, the next step was to make it competitive. Today, the sport of hot air ballooning tests the skill of the balloon's pilot in **accurately** guiding the balloon.

In a typical ballooning competition, targets are laid out over a **predetermined** course, and competitors drop marked weights over the targets. The winner is the pilot whose combined weights come closest to the targets over the entire course.

In the United States, the Balloon Federation of America (BFA) is the group that promotes and organizes events such as the U.S. National Hot Air Balloon Championship as well as local, state and regional competitions. The Hot Air Competition Division of the BFA makes and enforces the rules for these events. The rules are primarily designed to make sure that all the competing pilots are safe.

Iowan Bruce Comstock was a record six-time U.S. National Hot Air Balloon champion. He was inducted into the U.S. Ballooning Hall of Fame in 2006.

Hot air balloons float because the air in the balloon is lighter than the surrounding air. The air is heated by the controlled burning of fuel.

A hot air balloon pilot prepares for takeoff at the Fourth Putrajaya International Hot Air Balloon Fiesta in Malaysia.

Balloons in competition sometimes get a little too close for comfort.

Sidebar

Typically, ballooning competitions judge the ability of the pilot to guide the aircraft accurately over a marked course. There has also, however, been an ongoing competition over the decades that involves time and distance. In 2015, American Troy Bradley and Russian Leonid Tiukhtyaev took off from Japan in their helium-powered Kevlar balloon and landed just off the coast of Mexico. The historic flight broke the 37-year-old record for time afloat and shattered the 34-year-old record for distance by well over a 1,000 miles (1,609 km). The trans-Pacific flight lasted more than 160 hours and traveled nearly 7,000 miles (11,265 km).

Text-Dependent Questions

1. What one simple fact is at the heart of hot air ballooning?
2. What do competitors drop to measure the accuracy of their flight?
3. How is the winner determined in most ballooning accuracy competitions?

Research Project

Investigate to determine how many different types of hot air balloons there are in terms of the material used to make them, the fuel used to heat them, or the types of gas used to fly them. List the major differences or advantages of each kind you find.

Educational Video

Scan here to see a hot air balloon takeoff.

Gliding

Gliders are powerless aircraft that use naturally occurring air currents called thermals to remain airborne.

Words to Understand

currents: large portions of air moving in a certain direction.

evolved: coming forth gradually into being.

winch: a hauling or lifting device consisting of a rope, cable, or chain winding around a horizontal, rotating drum, turned by a crank or by motor or other power source.

Much like ballooning, gliding uses naturally occurring air **currents** to keep an unpowered aircraft airborne. Gliders, however, are heavier than air. The original goal of gliding was to stay airborne for as long as possible. In the 1920s, competitive gliding, therefore, was judged by distance, but once the gliders and pilots **evolved** to a point where they could stay airborne for days and travel thousands of miles, the competitions became tests of speed.

Gliders can be launched either by winch or by aerotow.

Today, gliders made of lightweight fiberglass rather than wood race over routes in the air, turning at designated points and returning to base. They are launched primarily by two methods. A launch by **winch** propels the glider from the ground into the air as the winch, at great speed, winds an attached cable. The other method is by aerotow, where a motorized airplane tows the glider through the air until the pilot releases the tow cable. Once airborne, the pilot uses columns of rising air in the lower atmosphere called thermals to maintain the glider's altitude.

Unlike a powered aircraft, where the pilot sits upright, seats in a glider's cockpit are reclined in order for the aircraft to be as streamlined as possible. The exteriors of gliders are seamless and smooth to maximize their aerodynamics.

Gliders used to be made of wood and metal components, but modern gliders are made primarily from carbon fiber and glass.

Sidebar

Enthusiasts interchangeably refer to the sport of gliding as soaring. Their machines can weigh from as little as 500 lbs (227 kg) up to as much as 2,000 lbs (907 kg). Although these machines are motorless, they are still regulated by the Federal Aviation Administration (FAA). Prospective pilots have to take lessons and study to pass the FAA written exam as well as the Private Pilot Glider test, which has oral and flying components. Solo glider pilots can be as young as 14 years old but are recommended to have at least 30 flights with a certified instructor before attempting a solo flight (with a student certificate). Pilots must be 16 to get a solo license.

Text-Dependent Questions

1. What keeps gliders airborne?
2. What two methods are used to launch gliders?
3. What agency regulates glider licenses?

Research Project

Gliders are launched from dedicated soaring sites. Identify a soaring site near you, and plan a visit. Interview several pilots to determine the three most common reasons they prefer to fly gliders.

Educational Video

Scan here to take to the skies in a gliding experience.

Hang Gliding and Paragliding

A common training technique for hang glider pilots in training is to fly in tandem with an experienced instructor.

Words to Understand

carbon fiber: a strong, stiff, thin fiber of nearly pure carbon, made by subjecting various organic raw materials to high temperatures, combined with synthetic resins, to produce a strong, lightweight material used in construction of aircraft and spacecraft.

harness: a set of straps that are used to connect a person to something (such as a parachute or a seat).

navigate: to travel on, over, or through an area or place.

A paraglider consists of a nylon canopy or wing called a ram-air airfoil with a pilot in a harness suspended beneath it.

Hang gliding has come a long way from the early attempts by the Chinese to jump from cliffs and towers strapped to large kites. Although the principle is essentially unchanged, pilots and designers today have a much better understanding of the science of flight. Modern hang gliders are still foot-launched by jumping off cliffs but are now made of **carbon fiber** or aluminum with sails of man-made material that can weigh as little as 45 lbs (20 kg). The pilot holds onto a triangular metal bar that extends below the sail of the hang glider then hangs beneath it as it sails through the air.

Competitive hang gliding is no longer based on length of flight but instead involves flying from a starting point to a designated end target using global positioning systems (GPS).

 Sidebar

As with many other types of flight, the weather plays a key part in whether or not to go hang gliding. Many hang gliding training programs include lessons in how to tell when the weather patterns are favorable or not. Responsible pilots will learn how to read wind speed and directional information and how to predict changes based on the types of clouds they see. Paragliders are especially subject to potential collapse from turbulence or high winds, which could cause rapid descent rates and high-speed impacts with the ground. Attempts to fly are generally considered to be safe when wind turbulence is smaller than the aircraft's lowest flight speed.

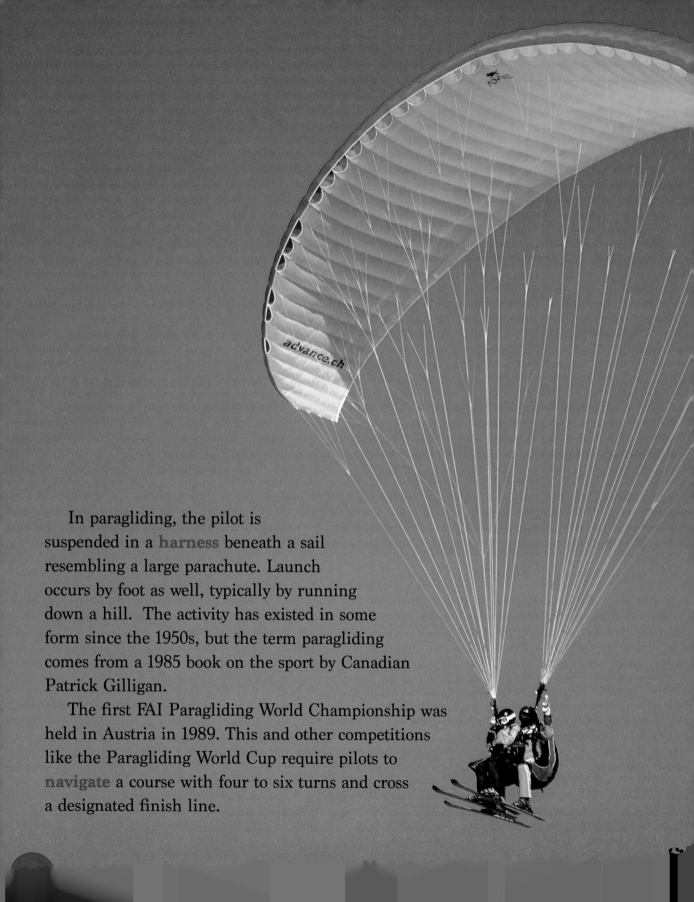

In paragliding, the pilot is suspended in a harness beneath a sail resembling a large parachute. Launch occurs by foot as well, typically by running down a hill. The activity has existed in some form since the 1950s, but the term paragliding comes from a 1985 book on the sport by Canadian Patrick Gilligan.

The first FAI Paragliding World Championship was held in Austria in 1989. This and other competitions like the Paragliding World Cup require pilots to navigate a course with four to six turns and cross a designated finish line.

Text-Dependent Questions

1. What did competitive hang gliding used to be based on?
2. How are paragliders typically launched?
3. Who came up with the term "paragliding"?

Research Project

Create a timeline highlighting the key moments in hang gliding and paragliding history. Investigate turn-of-the-century pioneers, such as Otto Lilienthal, Octave Chanute, and John Montgomery, and progress to the feats of Marcelo Prieto, Frank Brown and Rafael Saladini and beyond. Along with key moments from the sport's origins, also include at least two key developments or accomplishments in each decade from the 1960s to now.

Educational Video

Check out these gorgeous views from a virtual hang gliding experience.

Skydiving

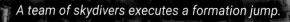

A team of skydivers executes a formation jump.

 ## Words to Understand

aerodynamic: of or having a shape that reduces the drag from air moving past.

disciplines: activities, exercises, or regimens that develop or improve a skill.

ripcord: a cord or wire that is pulled to open a parachute.

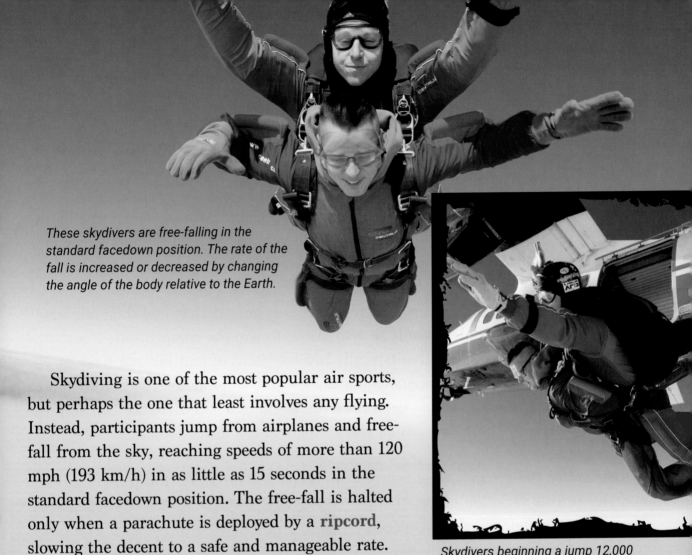

These skydivers are free-falling in the standard facedown position. The rate of the fall is increased or decreased by changing the angle of the body relative to the Earth.

Skydiving is one of the most popular air sports, but perhaps the one that least involves any flying. Instead, participants jump from airplanes and free-fall from the sky, reaching speeds of more than 120 mph (193 km/h) in as little as 15 seconds in the standard facedown position. The free-fall is halted only when a parachute is deployed by a **ripcord**, slowing the decent to a safe and manageable rate.

Skydivers beginning a jump 12,000 feet (3658 m) in the air.

Sidebar

The United States Parachuting Association has more than 36,000 members. In 2014, there were more than 3.2 million skydives in the United States, most of which were recreational jumps. In these attempts, just over 700 injuries were reported, along with 24 deaths. Given this very small percentage of less than 1%, the sport is very safe. The great majority of jumps are performed in tandem, where novice jumpers are strapped to experienced instructors during the jump.

In skydiving competitions, this speed can be increased by angling the body to be more **aerodynamic**. Competition **disciplines** in skydiving include:

- Accuracy—competitors aim for the center of a designated landing target.
- Angle flying—also known as flocking, tracking, or zooming, this is any jump where the competitor maintains an angle that is neither fully horizontal nor fully vertical to the ground. Various freestyle or acrobatic maneuvers can then be attempted and judged from these angles.
- BASE jumping—jumping from a fixed Building, Antenna, Span (bridge) or the Earth (cliff) with a parachute, BASE jumping is often called the world's most dangerous sport as it involves much lower altitudes than standard skydiving. Competitions are typically ones of landing accuracy.
- Cross-country—competitors open their parachutes immediately and then attempt to drift as far as possible (usually several miles) to win the competition.
- Formation—these are dives that typically involve teams of four but can have as many as eight, 10, or 16 jumpers who make geometric formations by holding onto each other in free-fall. Judges determine the winners. Then there are Big Way jumps, which can have as many as 400 jumpers in the formation.
- Freeflying—dives where competitors are completely vertical, either head or feet first toward the ground, where speeds can reach 200 mph (322 km/h).
- Style—in this variation of free-flying, competitors attain maximum speed by plunging headfirst and then execute a predetermined series of maneuvers that are judged for time and accuracy.
- Swooping—this is the term given to canopy piloting competitions based on the skills of the jumper after the parachute has opened. Competitors navigate courses and are scored for speed, distance, and accuracy.
- Skysurfing—divers perform and are judged on aerial acrobatics during the jump with a skateboard or snowboard deck attached to their feet.

This skydiver enjoys the exhilaration and rush of her very first skydive in tandem with her instructor.

Text-Dependent Questions

1. How long does it take a skydiver free-falling in standard position to reach a speed of 120 miles per hour (193 km/h)?
2. What is often called the world's most dangerous sport?
3. In what type of jump could a diver be completely vertical?

  # Research Project

Investigate how old you need to be to perform a skydive legally in the United States. How much instruction is required before you can make a tandem jump versus being able to jump on your own? How much does it cost to get licensed to skydive?

Educational Video

Watch this exciting skydiving experience.

Power Up

Powerless flight is difficult to control and at the mercy of the elements. The introduction of power to human flight negated the issues presented by the forces of gravity and drag by artificially improving those of thrust and lift. Humans have been soaring at high speed ever since.

Microlighting

In the United States, microlights, which are commonly called ultralights, weigh no more than 254 lbs (153 kg).

 ## Words to Understand

cockpit: the area in a boat, airplane, etc., where the pilot or driver sits.

fixed wing: of or relating to aircraft that derive lift from the motion of air over aerodynamically designed surfaces that are rigidly and permanently attached to the fuselage.

unregulated: not controlled or supervised by regulations or laws.

Microlight aviation is also frequently referred to as ultralight aviation and, in the United States, refers to **unregulated**, single-seat vehicles less than 254 lbs (153 kg). used for recreational flight. Worldwide, however, many countries do regulate microlights and classify both the electric and gas-powered versions as aircraft. Most are single flex wing aircraft with an open **cockpit** suspended below it that can carry a single person. The engine sits behind the cockpit.

There are also microlights with **fixed wings** resembling standard airplanes but which are categorized as microlights due to their weight and other specifications such as fuel capacity and speed capability.

Microlight pilot training courses are designed to make qualified pilots out of total beginners. This typically involves 10 to 12 days of intensive training, which includes both practical and theoretical exercises. The practical exercises include learning about the equipment, ground training, and both unpowered and powered solo flights. Theoretical exercises include flight theory, meteorology, navigation, aviation law, and safety.

In competitions such as the 2016 FAI World Microlight Championships, held in the UK, pilots competed in a number of tasks to test their skills. These included limited fuel tasks, navigation tasks, and precision tasks, where pilots were scored on their speed and accuracy.

Although unregulated in the United States, most other countries do classify microlights as aircraft and regulate them accordingly.

This powered paraglider would be classified as a microlight in most countries.

Microlights brought flying to the average person's backyard. Kits to build your own personal aircraft are available for less than $3,000.

Sidebar

Microlight aviation has made powered flight much more accessible to the general population. Flying airplanes for recreation was at one time a luxury for the wealthy or privileged. Microlights, however, are relatively affordable and can be bought and maintained for about the same as many people might spend on a motorcycle or small car. Many people even build their own microlights from kits that cost about $3,000. These aircraft can climb about 1,000 feet (305 m) per minute and fly more than 70 mph (113 km/h).

 ## Text-Dependent Questions

1. What is microlighting called in the United States?
2. Where were the 2016 FAI World Microlighting Championships held?
3. What are two of the components on which microlight pilots are scored in competitions?

 ## Research Project

Examine the differences between microlighting in the United States versus other countries in the world. Make a chart that compares the differences in definition, passenger capacity, weight, etc. in at least 10 different countries or regions.

 ## Educational Video

Hop inside a microlight to experience a landing.

Air Racing and Aerobatics

Chris Rushing (14) chases fellow pilot Fred Telling (89) during the T-6 Gold Medal race at the National Championship Air Races on September 16, 2012, near Reno, Nevada.

 ## Words to Understand

circuit: a series of performances, sports events, lectures, and so on, that are held or done at many different places.

inaugural: marking the beginning of a new venture, series, etc.

maneuvers: clever or skillful actions or movements.

A pilot races against the clock while maneuvering through a pylon course.

People have been racing airplanes since 1909, 6 years after the Wright brothers made their famous, but limited-success, first powered flight near Kitty Hawk, NC. There had been great improvements made in those 6 years, and in 1909, Glenn Curtiss from Buffalo, NY, won the **inaugural** Gordon Bennett Aviation Trophy when he flew 12 miles (19 km) in just under 16 minutes at the world's first major international flying race in Reims, France.

Today, professional air racers fly a **circuit** of international events in classes ranging from single-engine training aircraft to World War II-era jet fighters. Some races are timed one aircraft at a time through pylon courses, whereas others have all the planes racing through the pylons together from start to finish, like a car race.

 **Sidebar**

The Air Race World Championship is a multi-race series designed as a high-speed test of the skills of the world's best pilots through specially designed aerial racetracks. Pilots are awarded World Championship points for finishing in the top eight positions in each race. The first series was run in 2003 consisting of just two races. By 2007 the series had expanded to 12 races held around the world from Australia to the United States. After a 2010 crash in which the pilot was not seriously injured, the series took a 3-year hiatus to reevaluate safety precautions. It resumed in 2014. The 2015 champion Paul Bonhomme of England has 19 career wins and is a three-time series champion.

Speed is not the only game for competitive single-engine airplane pilots. Aerobatics involves performing **maneuvers** in the aircraft that are judged to determine the pilot with the best skills, who is named the winner. There are five categories of competition for powered aircraft, from the least difficult Primary, through Sportsman, Intermediate, Advanced, and Unlimited. Glider pilots compete in the non-power group in the Sportsman, Intermediate, and Unlimited categories.

Pilots fly up to four programs within each category:

- Known—A predetermined program flown all season long by all competitors
- Free—A program determined by individual pilots to showcase their skills
- Unknown—A program determined for each competition revealed to the pilots just hours before the competition
- 4-Minute Free—An invitation-only program designed to test the top pilots in each competition. Pilots are judged on the quality and precision of maneuvers, which include climbs, turns, rolls, slides, loops, spins, eights, and banks

Aerobatics teams are judged on synchronization and precision.

 **Text-Dependent Questions**

1. Who won the first Gordon Bennett Aviation Trophy?
2. Name the five categories of competition for powered aircraft.
3. What are the four possible programs within each category?

 **Research Project**

Write a one-page report on Russia's Svetlana Kapanina, who is considered to be the greatest female pilot in the world. Include facts about her background, training, awards, and accomplishments.

 Educational Video

Take your seat at an air show and watch daring pilots perform in this video.

Aeromodelling

Aeromodelling has a huge following in the United States. The Academy of Model Aeronautics, based in Muncie, IN, has more than 180,000 members nationwide.

Words to Understand

carbon dioxide: a gas that is produced when people and animals breathe out or when certain fuels are burned and that is used by plants for energy.

receiver: a device for converting signals (such as electromagnetic waves) into audio or visual form.

transmitter: a device that sends out radio or television signals.

Unmanned aircraft also have their place in the world of air sports. These include both scale models of existing aircraft, past or present, as well as aircraft that exist only in the aeromodelling world. These models come in three basic classes: free flight, which means that once launched, the aircraft cannot be controlled; control line, which are models that are attached by cables to a central point (usually held by the pilot) around which it is flown; radio control, in which the pilot uses a radio **transmitter** to send control signals to a **receiver** in the aircraft.

The FAI runs a World Cup season in aeromodelling from February to October, holding competitions in several categories within each class. World Cup events are held in several countries around the world. The first World Championships were held in 1960.

Model aircraft run on everything from rubber bands and **carbon dioxide** to jet fuel and batteries. Each category and class of aeromodelling has its own competitive circuit, where pilots compete in events based on speed, stunt flying, and racing, among others.

No other FAI discipline has more members than aeromodelling, which boasts more than a million people that participate in the sport worldwide.

Aeromodel pilots compete in events based on speed, stunt flying, and racing, among others.

An entrant controls his F3C aerobatic helicopter in a national aeromodelling race for nitro, gasoline, and electric remote control models on June 8, 2013, in Giannitsa, Greece.

 **Sidebar**

The Academy of Model Aeronautics (AMA) is the official body for aeromodelling in the United States. Based in Indiana, it charters more than 2,000 clubs with more than 180,000 members across 11 designated districts in the United States The AMA organizes the National Aeromodelling Championships, the largest model aviation competition in the world. The AMA has also awarded more than $1 million in scholarships to college-bound students pursuing technical careers.

Text-Dependent Questions

1. What are the three basic classes of model aircraft?
2. Name three items on which model aircraft can run.
3. Name three things that model aircraft competitions are based on.

Research Project

Assemble your own rubber propulsion model aircraft. Observe how the elastic motor works as well as the effects of declining torque on flight.

Educational Video

Go behind the scenes at an aeromodelling competition.

Helicopter Competition

Words to Understand

commission: a group of people who have been given the official job of finding information about something or controlling something.

ratify: to make a treaty, agreement, etc. official by signing it or voting for it.

rotorcraft: an aircraft whose lift is derived principally from rotating airfoils.

Helicopter competitions typically involve pilots racing either against the clock to complete a course or challenge or against each other.

The FAI sponsors a **rotorcraft** competition each year that encourages helicopter crews to issue worldwide challenges via the Internet. All crews that accept the challenge must agree to the date on which they will perform the challenge in their location. The FAI must **ratify** challenges, and an FAI representative must observe the challenge attempts. Approved results with supporting photographic evidence are then submitted to the official FAI judge, who determines the winner. Multiple challenges may be issued throughout the year, and at the end of each year, the FAI Rotorcraft **Commission** selects and presents a trophy to an overall winner.

The rapid rotation of a helicopter's rotor blades produce the necessary lift to achieve flight in these heavy machines.

In racing competitions, rotorcraft compete in two primary events: Parallel Fender and Parallel Slalom. In Parallel Fender, two helicopters race with the copilot in each holding a boat fender suspended from a rope. The pilot maneuvers the fender through gates set up on the ground. The pilot cannot see the fender and responds only to commands from the co-pilot. In Parallel Slalom, two helicopters race at the same time through a slalom course while this time suspending an open bucket of water, which once again the pilot cannot see. Points are deducted for time, missing gates, and lack of accuracy in landing the bucket on a 1 meter (3 foot) round table.

The FAI World Helicopter Championships are held every three years, and helicopters are among the aircraft that compete at the World Air Games, which take place every 4 years.

Helicopters used in air shows are designed for speed and maneuverability.

Sidebar

Outside of competition, helicopter pilots enjoy chasing records. American Edward Kasprowicz is the record holder for the fastest flight around the world in a helicopter. In August of 2008, he and a crew member circled the Earth, taking off from New York City on August 7 and landing there 11 days, 7 hours, and 5 minutes later. Kasprowicz's average speed was almost 90 mph (145 km/h), and they had to stop for gas more than 70 times.

Text-Dependent Questions

1. What organization sponsors an annual helicopter challenge competition?
2. Are there a set number of challenges that may be issued each year?
3. Who selects the overall winner each year?

Research Project

Search the Internet for video of helicopter competitions. Compile a list of the videos that best demonstrate the teamwork and precision piloting needed to be successful.

Educational Video

Join the Popular Rotocraft Association for a ride and closer look at their helicopters during their 50th anniversary gathering.

Want to Participate?

Check out some of these incredible places to either participate or watch these amazing air sports around the world.

Skydiving:

Palm Jurmeirah, Dubai

While Dubai is new to leading the drop zones in the world, the city now hosts one of the biggest annual international skydive championships. Setting it apart from the other top drop zones, Dubai is a city jump. Skydivers here fly over the Palm Jumeirah and get a mind-blowing view of the Persian Gulf and all of Dubai.

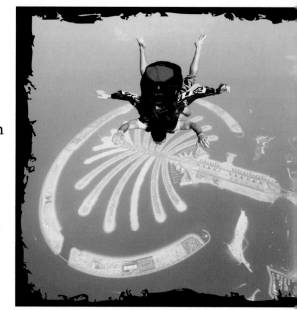

Palm Jurmeirah, Dubai

Here are more great places to skydive:

Fox Glacier, New Zealand

Fox Glacier is an 8-mile (13 km) long glacier located in the remote Westland Tai Poutini National Park on the West Coast of New Zealand's South Island.

Snohomish, WA, United States

Prepare for the sheer glory of the 360-degree panoramic view that surrounds skydivers at Snohomish, WA. From mountain to sea, this drop zone is renowned for being one of the most gorgeous in the United States.

Albuquerque, NM

Ballooning:

Albuquerque, NM

This American city is famous for its annual International Balloon Fiesta. The celebration brings hundreds of hot air balloon enthusiasts together in October every year for an amazing aerial experience.

Amazing venues across the globe to take a ride in the sky:

Serengeti, Tanzania

From high in the sky balloonists will look down on lions, giraffes, hippos, leopards, zebras, and wildebeest in the grassy plains of the Seronera River Valley.

Bagan, Myanmar

A journey over Bagan is truly awe-inspiring! Ride over the thousands of pagodas and ancient temples in the city that was once the capital of the first Myanmar empire. This aerial view is an exciting way to take in the scope of this captivating landscape.

Hang Gliding:

Interlaken, Switzerland
Interlaken has a long history as being a staple for adventure sports. Many hang gliders rate this as one of the most scenic drop zones in Europe. Free-falling in Interlaken awards views of Italy, France, Germany, and Austria stretching out past the snow-capped peaks of Jungfrau and the Matterhorn in the Alps.

Here are some more amazing hang gliding views:
Hautes Alpes, France
Check out the most amazing views while flying in the Alps! This is the biggest mountain range in Europe and provides an incredible backdrop for hang gliding.

Interlaken, Switzerland

Ölüdeniz, Fethiye, Turkey
Southern Turkey offers an unforgettable flight. Paragliders can see stunning blue lagoons underneath after taking off from Mount Babadag. Its 2,000 meters (2,187 yards) high!

Microlighting:

Victoria Falls, Zambia
This is a once-in-a-lifetime experience to take a microlight flight over this cascading wall of water then soar over Mosi oa Tunya National Park! Passengers can search for zebra, giraffes, and hippos from a unique vantage point.

Reno, NV

Air Racing:

Reno, NV

First held in 1964, the Reno Air Races feature multi-lap, multi-aircraft races. Reno is one of the few remaining venues for air racing as it holds this event, also referred to as the National Championship Air Races. This is a multiday event that takes place each September at the Reno Stead Airport a few miles north of Reno, NV. The event includes demonstrations by stunt pilots.

Want options? Check out the Red Bull Air Race! This competition was established in 2003. It's an international series of air races all across the globe. Competitors have to navigate challenging obstacle courses in cities such as Budapest, Las Vegas, Ascot, Abu Dhabi, and much more. At each venue, the top eight places earn World Championship points. The air racer with the most points at the end of the championship becomes Red Bull Air Race World Champion.

Further Reading:

Labrecque, Ellen. *Air Sports (Extreme Sports)*. United Kingdom: Raintree, 2015.

Loh-Hagan, Virginia. *Extreme Skydiving (Nailed It!)*. 45th Parallel Press, 2015.

Robinson Masters, Nancy. *How Does It Fly? Hot Air Balloon*. North Mankato, MN: Cherry Lake Publishing, 2013.

Internet Resources:

Balloon Federation of America
http://www.bfa.net/

Federal Aviation Administration
https://www.faa.gov/

World Air Sports Federation
http://www.fai.org/index.php

United States Parachute Association
http://www.uspa.org/

Photo Credits:

Video Credits:

Ballooning: http://x-qr.net/1GX7
Gliding: http://x-qr.net/1HcQ
Hang Gliding: http://x-qr.net/1Gxq
Microlighting: http://x-qr.net/1Go3
Aerobatics: http://x-qr.net/1H9V
Aeromodelling: http://x-qr.net/1Hi2
Helicopter Competitions: http://x-qr.net/1GV9
Skydiving: http://x-qr.net/1GP8

Author Bio:

Andrew Luke is a former journalist, reporting on both sports and general news for many years at television stations in various locations across the United States affiliated with NBC, CBS, and Fox. Prior to his journalism career, he worked with the Boston Red Sox Major League baseball team. An avid writer and sports enthusiast, he has authored 11 other books on sports topics. In his downtime Andrew enjoys family time with his wife and two young children and attending hockey and baseball games in his home city of Pittsburgh, PA.

Index:

In this index, page numbers in bold italic font indicate photos or videos.